How To Live In The Present Moment

Let Go Of The Past &

Stop Worrying About The Future

Matt Morris, CPCC

San Jose, CA

Oct. 3, 2020

Table Of Contents

Introduction

I want to thank you for downloading the book, "How To Live In The Present Moment: Let Go Of The Past & Stop Worrying About The Future".

This book contains proven steps and strategies on how to live in the present moment.

I begin the book taking you on a journey about how the past is important to learn from, but not something to hold on to and live for, transitioning into the future and talking about aspirations, while intertwining bits of the present into each of the chapters of the book, and then concluding with benefits and strategies of living in the present. An effective algorithm I've kept in the back of my mind for years now is the Past should consist of 10% of your thoughts, the Present 80%, and the Future 10%.

I spent much of my life living in the past and asking the question "Why me?" after my family and I were in a plane crash that killed my mother and almost killed me. It was difficult to let go of the past and move forward with my life. Years later it really hit me when I realized I was in my head *way* too much. I would be "having a conversation" with someone and at the same time I'd be worrying about things that were probably *never* going to happen; and thinking about things I'd already said or done, all at the same. I was totally missing out on the present moment, completely disengaged from the conversation.

I began to do a lot of personal development work, and slowly began to see how enlightening, beneficial, and peaceful it is to live in the present and simply enjoy every moment and be grateful for what is there, in that moment.

I'm not sure, but I imagine you want the ability to be more present and the ability to be more in the moment, in order to be less stressed and enjoy life more. Maybe you are too focused on events that have already happened, such as a break-up, or a stressful event at work; or maybe you are too busy planning things or multi-tasking that you can't simply stop and enjoy the moment.

Since I've lived primarily in the present moment over the past few years, I've learned that there are amazing benefits it. For instance, it has allowed me to have the most amazing conversations with others and connect at a level I'd never experienced before; it has allowed me to **not** be envious of what others have and instead be happy for them; and it has allowed me to accept the past and be excited for the future, and most importantly enjoy every moment.

Of course, the past is important to learn from, but not to live in. The future is important for your direction but not to be so consumed in that you can't enjoy the present. Ultimately, the present determines your future, so let's live in the present and enjoy the path to our future.

Thanks again for downloading this book, I hope you enjoy it!

Chapter 1
Pieces of Your Identity

A person's identity is created by past and present experiences, as well as aspirations or expectations of the future. One's history plays a significant role in how a person chooses to live life because it has contributed much to the formation of whom that person has become.

We will first take a brief look at why it's difficult to let go of the past and stop being anxious about the future. Following, we'll look at how rewarding it is to be in the present moment, and of course how to actually get there.

Having a better life is closely tied to your ability to let go of your past and not be too attached to what has already happened in your life. People have a very hard time releasing things because they think they'll crumble once these things are gone. This is why it's important to know that how you see yourself affects your decision on what to let go of.

Your History

It is what you create while still alive that gives you an idea of what has helped mold you into who you have become. You have a story, and some of the parts of your story are relevant to the improvement of your life. It consists of triumphs and failures, which are opportunities to learn from so that you can grow as an individual. These moments of triumph and failure are what makes life most rewarding or enriching and give the most room for expansion, improvement and growth.

Your past can either build you up or worsen your current condition. Many people have tough pasts and are able to use what they have experienced to learn in a positive way to better their current situation. At the same time, there are just as many people who can't get out the past and cannot seem to let go and move forward.

It is important to experience what you are going through, and not ignore what you are feeling for an extended period of time because the feelings will likely return. If you are feeling sad, accept it and be sad; the same goes if you're angry, be angry, and so forth.

Some believe that there is only one way to see things, when in every instance there are a number of ways to look at a situation. It is helpful to know that it is never too late to live a good life in the present, and shift your current view of your situation.

Be curious about your history. If you are struggling with something, exploring your past and assessing how you have gotten to this point in time will help bring you closer to the stage of letting go. Ask your parents, other relatives, or old friends from your past to tell you what they know about it. You can't let go of something you are not considerably knowledgeable about, so take this step and let the memories and knowledge of your ancestors become a teacher, not an enemy.

Let the past be your guide. The more you shun your history, the longer the process of letting go of the past will be. Remember that your past does not define you, but it is part of the path you've been on to get where you are today. You do not have to linger in the past, just realize that it is once was, and now you are in the present.

Your Identity

Throughout the book, it is necessary to relate your identity to your ability—and willingness—to let go of your past and stop worrying about what is to come. You may not be able to change what made you become the person you are today, but it is important to keep in mind that your current identity is who you are today, not yesterday. Many people spend their lives wondering and wandering aimlessly, without taking the time to stop and fully understand what it is they *really* want and then take small steps to reach these goals and get where they want to be.

Keep in mind that your past self does not exist anymore and your present self should realize that. Don't let the unchangeable, uncontrollable, and unpredictable govern your life and make you think you are less than you truly are. How you value yourself and your life should not be dependent on what has transpired or what has not yet occurred, but rather, who and what you are in this moment.

It is not an overnight transformation, but rather a constant transformation of state of mind to *remember* that you are here now, so enjoy it- wherever you are. With the right steps and a considerable degree of positivity, you will be able to easily access the present and be able to remain in it for a considerable amount of time.

So what should you do in order to move past the past or to avoid over-nurturing the future? The next chapter will look at different aspects of your past, which should be explored and most likely, let go of. Take time to absorb each and every aspect or area because the road to healing from the past is not always an easy or short one.

Putting the Pieces Together

You may know some of your identity's elements, but there's so much more you're missing if you're only trying to figure out who you are based on what you've done and what you can possibly achieve, rather than on what and who you presently are. Stop for a moment and listen to what's around you, and what is going on in your body. How is your posture? How is your breathing? What are you thinking?

Perhaps you are wondering how you can fully live in the present without being absorbed by regrets and worries. Everyone has struggles and the path toward a complete puzzle can be a long one, especially if you have already had a few broken pieces. Maybe you think it is not possible to be de-stressed about the past or anxiety-free about the future; and maybe you are on the verge of giving up.

Don't give up. Understand that the best is yet to come and know that you can start fresh at this very second by completely letting go of what you went through and considerably lessening your thoughts about tomorrow, next month, or next year. Stop for a moment, take a few deep breaths, and just be present.

Your goal may be to completely exist in the present so that you can find what you're actually looking for - possibly happiness and essentially, a better and more meaningful existence. Remember your identity is who you are today, right now, not who you were years ago or who you can possibly be years from now.

Inquiry 1: Take a moment to understand that yesterday is over, last year is over, this minute is over - the past is the past and can *not* change. The present is waiting for you to jump into and remain. I am longing for you to experience what it is like to live life in the present moment.

For the next 7 days, remind yourself to be in the present and if your thoughts shift in the future(and they will), shift your focus on where you're breathing and being in the moment. I encourage you to put sticky notes around your room, change your screen saver, or buy a necklace that you can use to a reminder to shift yourself back into the present.

Chapter 2
Past Relationships

One of the things that complicate a person's past and make it quite challenging to let go of things are relationships. Many would say that life would be simpler if people were spared from creating bonds with other individuals who have different beliefs and developing love or affection for such people. It's ironic to think that what can make a person's blood boil can also be the same thing he loves dearly.

This is why family, friends, and old or recent lovers make life quite colorful, both in pleasurable and appalling ways. Since the relationships in your life have such a strong impact of how you feel on a daily basis, detaching yourself from past issues, severing unhealthy relations, and letting go of what is not a big deal are clear musts. No one deserves to be chained to people and things that diminish your joy and peace in the present.

Family

Those closest to you can be the most dangerous. No one is saying that your mother, father, or siblings have plans to hurt you, but serious problems or issues in the immediate family are more probable to impact you than relationships that you don't have to think about or take care of on a daily basis. It's normal for families to undergo stressful and emotionally and mentally exhausting problems, but these don't have to last as long as most people allow them to. Issues that do last longer and therefore become more complex problems tend to create a cage around a person's heart.

You have to realize that what often cages you is not something beyond your control, especially if it stems from the past. Bitterness or grudges toward family members do not affect the recipient as much as they affect the one harboring them. It's time to let go of the pain you've been bottling up inside from a burnt relationship with for example your mother or a co-worker. Things may have not turned out the way you intended but that is out of your control. The *only* thing you can do now to ease your pain is to *forgive* and *move forward with your life.*

If a parent or sibling has realized their mistakes and are now making an effort to come back to you with renewed commitment and love, don't hesitate very long. In this case, remember once again that the present is what defines you, not the past. You can only let go of the past if you open your hands, eyes, and heart to the present. Empty yourself of the guilt and anger and let love and joy fill your heart and soul.

You can't choose the family you are born into, but you can choose who you become - despite what you've experienced or how you may have been treated by those whom you love. Forgiveness and letting go of the negative feelings or emotions may seem inconceivable at the moment, but don't shut your doors to such a need. It is possible to fully live in the present if you choose to take the next step and extend love to your family despite their shortcomings and mistakes.

Friends

It is much easier to lose a friend than a family member. For instance, you can lose friends if the relationships become strained by serious issues such as trust, loyalty, or reliability. Some friendships can last a lifetime because they're established on solid foundations, but some friendships are better ended, especially if they don't contribute to the improvement of your life or your personal growth. Friendship is a gift, not a burden where you *have* to constantly worry whether you're still friends with someone just because of brief misunderstandings.

A true friend will be there for you no matter what you're going through, no matter how strong the winds of adversity are, and no matter whom you are becoming — especially if it's a positive change for yourself. Your best friend, in particular, should accept you for who you are. He should value you to a degree that is comparable to the love of a family member.

Does your friend help you see yourself more clearly or is he fogging up the glass and not considering your feelings? How do his words and actions affect you? The people you keep in your life will significantly impact the way you live and how you think. Create bonds and friendships with people who care about you and love you even when you can't always help them when they're in a difficult situation.

Romantic Ties

It is safe to say that most people are more concerned about their love life than any other area of their life. It is understandable, though, because this aspect of your life affects you in so many ways.

Love has a way of changing people, either for the better or worse. Be careful with who you fall in love with because he or she gains the power to lift you up or crush your spirit. Let the pain of a past romantic relationship teach you what you should *not* do in your current and future relationships.

Mistakes are the best teachers. Even if you have gone through several failed relationships, it doesn't mean that your current one is also doomed to fail. In the same way that you are not defined by your past identity, your present relationship also is not tied to the past. It is common for relationships to be negatively impacted by things that shouldn't even be there in the first place. It's not healthy to continue to focus on "should haves" or "what ifs", when there is so much richness in what there already is.

Career or Work-Related Relationships

Even your relationship with previous employers or co-workers affects your life considerably. One of the primary reasons why this is the case is that they are connected to the progress of your career. People in their prime are quite concerned about such a relationship because they have also invested a portion of their heart into each and every company they have worked in.

In nearly every company, the "crab mentality," which is basically the desire to get higher in the ladder even at the expense of someone else's welfare or happiness, is very common. It's natural for a person to get promoted and sometimes, he lets his desire get the best of him, making him insensitive to the needs of others. Friendships are destroyed as trust is ruined at the price of advancing in your career. Bitterness and a strong hesitation to withhold forgiveness are also common, tainting a once-healthy working environment.

You have the choice of either letting your co-workers negative actions consume your thoughts and energy by allowing their past actions to linger in your mind and heart, or you have the choice to just let it go. The point is to simply let your co-worker live her life so that you can also allow yourself the same freedom. Many people miss out on many things happening in their current career because of their attachment to past betrayals and mistakes. Don't trap your own career in the past because you have the potential to become more once you

11

release the history.

The next section of the book will further discuss the importance of letting go and some of the essential factors affecting its accomplishment. Once again, no matter what type of relationship you're hung up on, or whatever form of mistake or betrayal was done in the past, don't let it consume your present because the past is over and there is no going back, so continue moving forward.

Inquiry 2: Take a moment to ponder. Are there people or things that are bringing your life down - taking away from your joy? What or who are they? How can you either change your perspective or cut these from your life? What do they add to your life? What do they take away from your life and your ability to be present?

Chapter 3
Letting it All Go

It is human nature to become too attached to things or people, which can often lead to unhealthy addictions. The first step to letting go is the desire to move on from the past, and notice what role it is playing by keeping this past issue in your life.

Next, you'll have to change your perspective of the situation. This can be achieved with the help of a "quiet time" or meditation. Crying your frustrations and pain away may also be an effective way to move away from a painful past. Fully relive this experience in your mind to keep forward and put this past behind you.

How willing you are to forgive *yourself* and *others* for the things that happened in the past? It is easier said than done, and you're not alone in this. Let's take a look at highly effective ways that this can be accomplished.

A Change of Perspective

The eyes are considered to be the windows to the soul, not only because you can see a person's inner being through the eyes, but because one's perspective also heavily impacts the way he lives his life and how tight he's gripping onto the past. The lenses you use to view the world, your circumstances, and yourself *can* be changed. It's not really possible to *forget* about the past, but if you are able to develop a new way of looking at it, you will feel a huge weight lifted off your shoulders.

Looking at your past as an enemy can be counterproductive, especially if this perspective only leads you to feelings of resentment or guilt. It is much worse when things happened that are out of your control and *you* are taking the blame.

13

You may not be able to change your circumstances, but you can change the way you see things. If you can find a way to look at this experience as an opportunity to grow and learn from, it will not only increase your present strength, but it will make the past seem less significant.

Pain strengthens people because it's only through hard work and suffering that you can develop strong callouses against present and future trials or problems. Develop the willpower to smile or laugh at your past no matter how dark it was. For example, if your boss talked down to you when you made a mistake—making you feel less confident and quite emotionally and mentally fragile in certain instances—it's necessary to look at that experience in a different light. Maybe take the perspective of placing less importance of others' opinions about you.

It is also important to challenge those beliefs and assumptions that anyone who doubted you placed in your mind. Go out and test them in the real world and notice that you are fully capable of getting the results you want, whether it be getting a job you desire, or getting a romantic partner of your choice. Of course, much in life is a numbers game, so the more you do it, naturally the better you will get.

Once you begin to look at your past differently, new doors will open, allowing you to get closer to letting go of the things that only cause you pain. Anger, fear, and worry only blur your assessment of things, so it's better to take a look at the past more carefully and with an open mind.

- What is important about this event in my past?

- What have I learned about myself?

- What do I want now?

The answers to these questions will only come to those who earnestly and calmly seek them. Negative emotions and resentment-filled lenses will only cause you to suffer and remain stagnant.

Meditation

When you meditate, you empty yourself of all the things that are unhelpful to the development of inner peace. Meditation isn't limited to precise stretches, body positions, proper breathing, and a completely peaceful environment. Meditation can be done inside your room or even your office.

Take time to think about the life you've been given. Let the past flow out of your system as you take deep breaths and let your mind wander into places where you've prohibited it to explore. It is best to close your eyes when you do this because it will prevent your mind from external distractions. Meditation gurus suggest having a mantra when you meditate. The most common one is repeating "om" in your mind as you begin to relax and de-stress.

Meditation is one of the best ways to de-stress. As you meditate and allow your tensions to be released from your system, you'll be able to think more clearly. Meditation allows people to clear their mind and learn things about themselves. For example, you may use it to be able to realize why certain feelings came up during a particular event, why you approached a problem the way you did, what made you say what you said, and even get clear on what you want for each day. The fact is that you can solve many of your own problems if you're in the right state of mind. If you're not stressed, your mind will be more clear and creative. You'll have time to process everything and encourage yourself to naturally take the next step toward letting go of the past.

Know what's in your mind and heart so that you'll also know what you should do after your "quiet time." Carl Jung once said, "Your vision will become clear only when you can look into your own heart. Who looks outside, dreams; who looks inside, awakes."

As yoga experts claim, the condition of the body affects the condition of the mind and vice-versa. Take care of yourself by balancing your time. Don't immerse yourself in your work, school, or spend too much time doing one thing.

If you want more information on how to get started with Yoga, I recommend Shivani Gupta's Meditation book. It's a simple guide to get started with meditation and talks about styles you can add to your daily practice for inner peace and happiness.

Tears of Healing

Crying has a way of easing tension, and releasing negative energy and emotions from your body. Biologically speaking, crying also releases toxins in the body. People who cry when they need to often feel much better afterward.

Yes, your past is as cruel and merciless as you think, but isn't your present relatively better? The sun will still rise and birds will keep on chirping. Let your tears fall so that your grief can flow out of your body in a physical manner as well as an emotional and mental one.

Telling yourself to not cry is cruelty because you're not designed to just forget your pain by sheer will power. Cry it out and shout if necessary, even if you're only doing it once.

Sometimes, crying once is enough to help you move many steps closer to emotional and mental healing because you have allowed yourself to live naturally and react to your frustrations.

Forgive Yourself

Forgiveness directed toward the self proves to be much more complicated than you think being that you are your greatest critic and judge. How many times have you made a mistake and how many times have you missed opportunities because of your own fear and insecurities? Your greatest enemy is yourself and that hinders you from living the life you want.

Forgiveness is important because it's one of the keys that allow you to get "unstuck" and move forward in your life. It may not be the same as forgetting a fault, but it's more than enough to push you forward and live a life that brings joy to yourself and to others. Hesitation to forgive yourself limits your thoughts and actions, worsening your perception of your self.

If you can't forgive yourself, you won't be able to spread your own wings. The fact is that you'll still make mistakes and you'll still get hurt, but forgiveness enables you to be fully charged up to face new challenges because you've embraced the fact that you're just human, you make mistakes- as does everybody else, and it's not always your fault when things don't turn out the way you want them to. Before you can extend forgiveness to others, you must start with yourself because it's hard to give something you don't have.

Forgive Others

Since bitterness and grudges are among the things that primarily make up your chain to the past, choosing to forgive and love those who have hurt or disappointed you will significantly make letting go easier. When you forgive others, as you forgive yourself, you're using this power to heal wounds and address discord. Further, your forgiveness will set you free.

Many times people have difficulty forgiving someone because they themselves have never been forgiven for the things they've done against someone else. This is an unfair, and often-unavoidable route in a relationship. It's easier to just let the pain go by forgiving. Prolonging the anger and hatred will only cause you more built-up stress and complication.

You may want to "teach them a lesson" for betraying you and when issues regarding trust arise, where extending forgiveness becomes seemingly impossible. However, take a look at the situation once again. In reality, you would be the one who's losing more in this silent and prolonged war; the one who's wasting time stressing and thinking of the loss instead of forgiving and moving on.

Life is short, even though your past may seem to span hundreds of years because of the resentment attached to it. If you're not going to forgive yourself and others, a better life will be even further for you to grasp. It's true that your relationship with these people may no longer be the same as before, but the present is the perfect time to mend wounds—no matter how deep they are—and create healthy relationships.

The past is not the only thing negatively affecting your life in the present. The future is also a contributor to your woes or worries, so it's also advisable to explore why things that have not transpired yet already cause you to worry and get stressed out in the present. The next chapter discusses how thoughts about the future can work against your pursuit of a better life.

Inquiry 3: Take a moment to relax and forgive yourself from has happened in the past. Take a deep breath and as you exhale, send the past on its way because it is over. Next, take a moment to forgive others for what they have done to you so that you can set yourself free.

Chapter 4
Future Considerations Over-Planned

Insurance companies may enjoy the fact that most people are quite concerned about their futures. In this aspect, it is wise to have something prepared in case you get into an accident. However, in order to live in a way that's helpful to you and your loved ones, it's best to shift your focus on the present. You may already be wondering how you can actually stop worrying about the future. Let's take a look at the following points to have a better idea of what you can do.

The Future Is Not Controllable

If you believe in a higher being or a deity, you'll claim that only God, Allah, or some other god can control what happens in the future. If you don't adhere to any religious beliefs, you'll still probably think that controlling the future is impossible. You can't control what will be on the front page of the news a week from now, and you can't control who will win a million dollars in a Las Vegas slot machine tomorrow.

The only thing you can control is the present and even this period is limited to what's within your reach or influence. Many people worry and get frustrated because they're afraid that their job interview the next day may not turn out the way they need it to. Some are scared that they may not get the promotion they need to be able to pay off their mortgages and other bills. Others are worried about their unfinished work project, which is due tomorrow.

Worries stem from a lack of control over the things that we want to have control over. This is why some opt to explore the supernatural or try to tap into what they think can help them change the future for their own benefit. From these actions, one can also safely assume that worries can even originate from selfishness. You're worried about your own life and welfare that you forget that current circumstances require your full attention.

Worries can also stem from a concern for others. You may be worried about your child's future or your marriage's future. These worries naturally occur to most people, but you can train yourself to not think about them and just concentrate on living in the present. A small portion of the worry can be used as motivation and create urgency to get the job done, but don't allow it to overpower where you are in the present. Instead, use your energy and abilities to make the present a better one because thinking about the future and trying to control it will only tax your will and joy.

The Future Is Not Predictable

You cannot control the future because you cannot predict it. Many people go to fortune-tellers or to people who claim they can foresee what's going to happen. If you've read much of the literature available today regarding predicting the future, you will see that most, if not all, predictions are a hoax. No matter how many years of experience someone has in developing his or her self-claimed "gifts" of predicting the future, nothing is set in stone.

Remember that your plans and goals for the future are still written on sand. They can be washed away by the circumstances that you will eventually face; they can be altered by other factors such as changes in your desires or realizations regarding your purpose in life. You can't even honestly predict exactly what you're going to do tomorrow or what your boss will tell you regarding your job.

That's just it: you're not sure what the future holds. No matter how long people try to think about it, predictions about the future will remain what they are: predictions. As you let go of your past due to the realization that you *can't* change it, remember that despite the unpredictability of the future, you *can* still change what it may become if you focus on living well in the present.

The Future Is Not the Enemy

Generally, people are good at being pessimistic and they love to exaggerate many possible circumstances in their lives. Thoughts such as, "I won't be able to graduate from college because Advanced Chemistry is so hard," represent only a small part of what people—particularly the relatively young ones—are worried about. Some may even think that they won't be able to meet a great person to marry because they've been looking and they haven't been able to find one. Others are primarily concerned about their career and they think that they'll just be stuck in whatever position they're in because they lack the necessary skills and know-how to move up the ladder.

The future has become a common enemy of many individuals and this is clearly unhelpful and unnecessary because the future doesn't have any sides. It's neither for the bad nor the good. It doesn't have a

22

will of its own, so it can't actually plot any evil scheme against you. It's just an unpredictable period of time and is determined by the actions and choices we make in the present.

In most cases, though, the future is not as bad as you think it'll be. Once you're there in the interview room, you realize that you're able to answer the employer's questions with confidence and certainty. Once you submit that carefully made project or paper, you'll see that your teacher appreciates the hard work that's clearly seen in how meticulously you accomplished the assignment. Once you're in the exam, you'll see most of the questions about chemicals and compounds are not gibberish, but can actually be answered if careful calculations and considerations are made.

You should also remember that what you're expecting to happen will most likely happen if you've invested much energy in thinking that things will unfold in such a way. As Rhonda Byrne says in *The Secret*, "Your thoughts become things." If you expect the worst, the worst may materialize itself. However, if you choose to think positively and just let peace reign in your heart in the present, you'll have a better perspective for the future.

Some use the present to soothe the future with visualization techniques. For example, visualizing being at an interview and experiencing how it would feel to be there, what the interviewer might ask you and how you'd like to respond will ease anxiety and tension. As Allyson Felix, the 2012 Olympic Gold Medalist said, "I am a big believer in visualization. I run through my races mentally so that I feel even more prepared." It's once again about perspective. You'll see what you want to see, and even though you can't predict the future, using the present to visualize will surely decrease anxiety and worry for the future.

You may have several enemies, but the future isn't one of them. Your future is dependent on what you're doing at the moment; so stop worrying about it because these efforts are pointless. What helps make your future a brighter one is if you'll make the decision today to *choose* to be happy and *thankful* for the present, and just let the future *be*.

Healthy Planning for the Future

No one's telling you to stop preparing for the future altogether, but *thinking* about the future and *worrying* about it are clearly two different things. You can plan for your future in a healthy way, which won't cause you to get sucked into a seemingly inescapable cycle of worry, disappointment, fear, and sorrow. As mentioned previously, one thing that I've found very useful is using the 80/20 rule – having the Present consume 80% of my thought and feelings, with the Past taking up 10%, and the Future being the other 10%. Of course, this can't be an exact measurement, but it is a good ballpark figure that I've found works to remain present, and still be aware of the past and future.

Applying for insurance policies is among the most practical and advisable ways to prepare for the future because these don't require much thinking. You just have to sign a few documents after learning about the conditions and provisions of the policy. A certain amount of money will be deducted from your monthly pay—depending on your terms of payment—and you can just focus on other present concerns. This will allow peace-of-mind by not having to worry about the "what-ifs" of the future.

Most families even start saving money for the future. Saving money is a healthy way of managing current wealth so that there's money for a highly probable future, including college, retirement, or an overseas vacation. As you can see, there are ways you can prepare for the future without stressing over each and every detail. You should not *worry* about what degree your child will get or what type of people he'll meet in college because these are uncontrollable factors. You can influence his decisions in college, but ultimately it is his choice.

Another example that cause stress and worry is watching the evening news. 99% of the things on the news will not and do not affect us, but instead cause anxiety and worry for the future, which again is not under our control. If something comes up that is important for us, we will hear about it through social media (Facebook, Twitter, Email, Yahoo, the list goes on) or through word of mouth.

Inquiry 4: What is something you are currently worrying about? Think about whether you can control it or not. How important is it for you to hold onto this worry?

For the next week, my request is for you to give yourself permission to let go of this worry. Whenever it comes up, jump back into the present and focus on your breathing. If you need reminders (e.g. sticky notes, a piece of jewelry, or adding it to your daily

calendar, etc.) go ahead and put those in place. Commit to letting go of the worry.

In one week, check back in and see how that worry is. How did it feel when you weren't worrying about it? What's changed since letting go of that worry?

Chapter 5
The Gift of the Present

Many successful individuals promote the importance of living in the present including: Jim Rohn, Bill Cosby, and Jimmy Carter. They understand that the present moment is the only time they can control. They don't seem rushed, and still get a lot done. Knowing and understanding this gives you the ability to *listen* to what is being said, or fully enjoy the *taste* of a meal or the *sound* of a piece of music. These are a few of the advantages of being in the present moment.

A full focus on the present is a prerequisite to triumph, to a more meaningful and wonderful existence. People are very limited and they have a tendency to try and exceed these limitations because they're unaware that such boundaries exist. Many people think they're good at multitasking, but eventually learn that some things just *can't* be done simultaneously. For example, if you are attempting to have an engaging conversation on the phone and listening intently, while checking and reading your email, you are missing out on the experience of both because neither will have your full attention. You'll miss details, and the quality of both will be decreased.

You can't focus on the present and fully see its beauty if you're too hung-up on the past or too focused on the future. Essentially, you can't completely enjoy the *gift of the present* if you're filled with regret and worry.

Here are some of the reasons why it's difficult to get out of the vicious cycle of overthinking, regretting, and worrying about the past and the future:

The Illusion of Time

There's a belief that the time does not really exist; that there's only a passing of time and only the past and future should receive an individual's attention and concern. This belief makes it difficult in helping someone to truly exist completely in the present.

There is a present. Eckhart Tolle, the author of the widely recognized book, *Power of Now* stated, "Observe that the future is usually imagined as either better or worse than the present. If the future is better, it gives you hope or pleasurable anticipation. If it is worse, it creates anxiety. Both are illusions." It's easy for people to think about or remember the past and try to predict the future, but only few do allot a portion of their day to stop and think of where they are in the moment.

The present may only be accurately defined using the definition of the past and the future, even though it's quite detached from the other two time periods. You must overcome the illusion of time and realize that you're more than the sum of your past and the predictions of your future. Once you see the beauty of the present - the only reality that is here, in *this moment* - you won't be submerged in anxiety for the future, or guilt from the past.

Living in an Illusion

Mitch Albom wrote a very inspiring and thought-provoking novel entitled "The Time Keeper." In this book, he illustrated through his words the pitfalls of being overly concerned about time and counting the seconds instead of living them. The three main characters in the novel suffered much because of their attachment to time, but were able to find salvation in the end by realizing that what's important is to enjoy each and every second of your life doing what you can and should do, and spending your life with the ones you love.

Time is an illusion. Years ago, people lived simply and were quite happy because instead of being concerned of the time lost, they focused on the time they still had; the time they could use to improve themselves and be a positive contribution to society. Many of the greatest inventions in history were created because of pioneers and inventors who chose to live in the present and not linger in past mistakes or worry much about the future.

Thomas Edison had to try many materials and had to face numerous failures before he was able to invent the incandescent light bulb. Alexander Graham Bell failed at several things including the "flying machine"- before inventing the telephone. What if these brilliant men only focused on their past failures and mistakes?

You get closer to your goal if you focus on the tasks at hand. Look at the present and do not worry about how your past still clings to a part of your identity or how your future will unfold one day. When you're immersed in the present, this present will eventually be a wonderful memory of the past and will be the catalyst to creating a better future.

Listen to Yourself, Listen to Your Life

It is common for people to have a really hard time *living in the present* because they are too busy talking and thinking. Only few have actually developed great listening skills, enabling them to see, realize, and appreciate what they have before them. As many leaders claim, those who listen gain more than those who talk.

Living in the present requires an understanding of *who you are* in the present and *where your life is* right now. Since you are no longer focused on the passing of time—what the past has offered and what the future has in store—develop the habit of listening to yourself and learning about your own life. It's relatively easy for most to listen to others and learn from their lives, but it takes a deeper level of awareness and an even greater level of commitment to be able to listen to yourself and learn from your own current circumstances.

You won't be able to listen to yourself think if you're in the middle of the heavy traffic, in a crowded market, or while working. As discussed earlier in the book, it's important for you to set a "quiet time"; a time where you can concentrate on becoming sensitive to your own emotional, mental, and even spiritual needs. As you meditate, notice your breathing patterns and what your body is telling you. The silence will allow you to explore what you normally can't access in the midst of the noise and turmoil. When you choose to listen to yourself through meditation, you are choosing to be more aware of the present moment and can gain access the beauty within.

Unnecessary Imagining and Conceptualizing

People love to plan; and planners are particularly in high demand toward the end of each year to the first quarter of the following year. Many people use their smart phones to take note of reminders, meetings, and other activities so that they won't forget their other responsibilities and commitments. You can say that a significant portion of people's time is spent planning for things; setting deadlines, parties, and other events.

The youth are particularly prone to such a planning frenzy. Those who are entering college and those who are about to head off to join the corporate world are so—and most likely, too—fond of planning. There are many disadvantages of *excessive planning*, and one of them is to *miss out on what's currently happening in your life*. Let's say you're on a business trip, and even while you're on the trip, you've already started thinking and planning for another one the following week, missing out on the entire experience.

Your mind is not where it should be when you constantly plan, imagine, or conceptualize your life. Life is one big journey and it shouldn't only be filled with plans that only eventually become a distraction for another plan. Yes, planning for the future is important, but when it becomes excessive, you miss out on the present.

After all, what you're ultimately looking for is joy and satisfaction, right? These come from a sense of accomplishment; a feeling that you've done your best to achieve your goal and have consequently helped yourself and others. Plans don't change lives, actions do. Plans are just one of the steps to achieve your goals.

Enjoy the Present

Even though more than a couple of babies are born every second around the globe, many parents still suffer from losing a child due to miscarriages and illnesses that particularly target premature babies. Someone dies every second, either from accidents, murders, suicide, or terminal illnesses. These are examples of how short life can be and a reminder of how important it is to enjoy what you have right now, the present.

Not everyone is given the privilege of spending every day with loved ones. Many have to watch their husbands or fathers leave every year to serve in the army; to serve the nation. Others have work obligations that require spouses to be across the globe for a few weeks or months each year. Some people don't even get to spend more than a few years with their family and friends due to tragic accidents. The point is to cherish the moments you do have with loved ones because you never know if you will see them tomorrow.

You can't control the future and you can't change the past. No matter how much people want it, they can't predict what will happen in the next few seconds, minutes, hours, days, weeks, months, and years. There are things that are beyond your control not because life's punishing you, but because it wants you to see that the unpredictability and the fragility of your existence makes life that much more precious. Every second becomes more beautiful because it may be the last, so learn to enjoy the present because it is a gift.

If you're still unsure of what you should do to fully enjoy the present because you're still in the process of letting go of the past; or perhaps training yourself to stop worrying or feeling anxious about the future, the next chapter provides simple and effective steps on how to fully be in the present. Moving on from the past may require a longer time than you think, but it's not exactly a process that should be rushed. It may require more than a couple of night's efforts to fully commit to living in the present, but keep moving forward because the internal rewards are astounding.

Inquiry 5: Take a moment to relax. Congratulate yourself for reaching this point in the book.

Now, think of all the things you have to get done today, and tomorrow, and the rest of this week. How many thoughts are racing though your mind right now? How many times a day do you attempt to do several things at once?

My request for you is to go *one day without multitasking,* to experience it. This is not to decrease your productivity, but instead to see the beauty in every single thing we do. Often times, you will be more productive and far more efficient when you take the moment to do just one thing at a time.

Be fully immersed in the one activity you are doing, without being distracted. For example, if you are having a conversation at lunch and your cell phone buzzes, don't text or answer the phone(or simply keep your phone on silent); for each food you eat actually *taste it* instead of viewing Facebook or text messages on your phone; or even if you doing a chore, for instance the laundry, be fully immersed in the activity using your senses in the present moment-instead of thinking about what happened earlier that day or what else you need to be doing – Think about, the smell in the air, the texture of the clothes, feel how your arms move when you're placing the laundry in the washing machine. Just be in the moment.

You may find this request completely ridiculous or you may find it absolutely refreshing, but either way you won't know how it is until you experience it. So go ahead and try it, just for a day.

Chapter 6
Using Time Wisely

Everyone has 24 hours a day and seven days a week, so you can't complain that others have more time than you. Some are able to better manage themselves, allotting just the right amount of time each day for every activity. They're also able to simultaneously ignore the troubling moments of their past and choose to not focus on the unpredictable and uncontrollable future.

These people use their time wisely. They are aware of the things that complete the puzzle of life - things that stem from being conscious of the present. They know that they are in the present and that's enough knowledge for them to move on from the past and be excited for the future without letting themselves undergo pressure and stress. As introduced in the first section of the book, everyone's trying to complete his or her own life puzzle. The challenge is figuring out what pieces actually constitute the puzzle.

Completing the Puzzle of Life

The puzzle of life is made up of the past, present, and future. Experiences and memories accumulate from the past and are continuously gained in the present, while you're creating your future. Future goals and considerations affect one's decisions in the present and your actions and thoughts in the moment are affected by past mistakes and emotions attached to your own history.

This is the puzzle of life. How you manage these elements define who you are. You're either living in the past, present, or future and you *can't* exist in these three time periods at the same time. Your life is where your heart and mind are. Take a look at yourself at the moment. Look at your present and, at this moment, think about where you are in life right now. Think about who you have become. Are you on your way toward a better life? And do your actions and thoughts remain consistent with your desire to reach your goal?

Completing the puzzle of life demands a deeper awareness of your identity and a consistent desire to know where you are in the timeline. You can't complete the puzzle if you don't acknowledge the importance of the most important piece of the puzzle: the present or, as Eckhart Tolle calls it, "the Now". To know where you are and where your energy is flowing is just the beginning to completing your puzzle and existing in the present.

Ways to Fully Enjoy and Maximize the Present

Many are just partly enjoying the gift of the present. Some are able to become fully aware of the present, and others take a relatively long time to get to that state. No matter what your pace is, though, simply having the will to rediscover your existence and identify are commendable efforts. Here are some of the ways in which you can fully enjoy and maximize the present.

Discover Yourself Daily

You change every day. Physiologically speaking, all the cells in your body change constantly and in just 7 years, you're no longer the same person on a molecular or cellular level. Your body moves forward from the past and once you reach 70, you'll have changed 10 times. If your physical body can move forward, then surely your mind and heart can do the same.

Even if we are the ones inhabiting our bodies, it doesn't automatically and necessarily mean that we already know every single detail about ourselves. You may have not memorized every single organ or part of your body, but the idea being proposed here is that people are only at the tip of the iceberg when it comes to being familiar with *whom* they actually are. This leaves much room for exploration and the other pieces of your identity can be found in your subconscious.

There are times when the subconscious lets out bits of information that we have stored in our mind; things that may help us become more familiar with who we are and what we dream to be. The mind is often considered an untapped well of memories and information; and yet in this hectic world, it is not always easy to find time to explore the mind extensively, although it is imperative to accessing answers. This is why it's important to set time on the side for "quiet-time" or meditation, to allow you to connect or reconnect with who you are becoming and what you want.

As you discover more of yourself, you'll be able to see things from a new perspective because you are slowly becoming more familiar with who you are—how you think and how you interpret various things. You are slowly transforming into a person who can contribute much more to the people you love.

Further, since you are now aware of what your past has developed or created in you, you can learn and take the opportunity to grow from your painful experiences and cease resenting them.

Learn from Present Mistakes and Learn to Laugh at Them

Learning and laughter *can* and *should* work hand-in-hand. It's easier to learn from something if you are enjoying the learning process. Although your past experiences can be more uncomfortable than your overly strict and merciless teacher back in high school, it is often the most effective educator. Therefore, embrace the fact that these are your experiences and they have and will help mold you into a stronger and more persevering person today.

Tony Robbins says it well with, "Go out and screw up. You're going to anyway so you might as well enjoy the process. Take the opportunity to learn from your mistakes; find the cause of your problem and eliminate it. Don't try to be perfect, just be an excellent example of being human."

Laugh about the mistakes you once made. You can remember when you were a nervous wreck in a job interview or when you completely choked when you tried to talk to that person you found very attractive or when you were beet red as you were called in front of the class to answer a math equation. Smile now, and laugh.

These events in your life certainly were embarrassing at the time, but the ability to laugh at them in retrospect is powerful and will give you fuel to keep moving forward. You can't let failure stop you or you will never push yourself. Continue to push because you believe in your vision, and success will follow. Let your experiences be an opportunity to grow and learn.

Develop a Hobby

Some say hobbies help define people. Hobbies are activities that help you get out of a routine life and into a more spontaneous existence. Finding new hobbies every now and then or really immersing yourself in your current hobbies will help keep things interesting and fun. For instance, many people who seek out hobbies such as rock climbing and yoga are more prone to being in the present, as it is necessary to be aware of what the body and mind are doing while climbing or holding a position.

Art offers various avenues for those who want to explore their artistic abilities. You can sketch, paint, and sculpt anything you can conceive and through your creations, you'll also see the extent of your current abilities and what you can still work on to improve your talents. Art is limitless and it's a great way to use the present moment to explore your thoughts, beliefs, feelings, and desires. Further, people can see the depth and beauty of your life through your art.

Listen to Music with Positive Messages

Listen to music that can help soothe your mind and aid you as you discover more of yourself. With numerous genres available, you'll surely find something that can create an ambience conducive to meditation.

Many prefer to listen to classical music and ambient nature sounds as they meditate daily. The complex arrangement of the musical notes helps the mind process thoughts more easily. Listening to Mozart, Pachelbel, Beethoven, Tchaikovsky, and many other renowned classical composers, has a tendency to simplify the process of self-discovery and make your time in the present more productive.

Music has the power to heal and is also another form of art, which you can work with as you explore your identity in the present. Music is, after all, a frequent companion of many students as they study and by urban travelers as they walk around the bustling metropolis. Music is a reliable and helpful companion for those who want to enjoy the present more.

Spend More Time with Your Loved Ones

Maybe you've heard the saying that "Love is spelled T-I-M-E." This short, yet meaningful statement is a condensed message of children to their parents, of parents to their adult children, and of people to their friends. What keeps you busy every day is where your heart is.

As Steve Jobs put it, "My favorite things in life don't cost any money. It's really clear that the most precious resource we all have is time." Sadly, not many recognize this because people are too busy earning money for themselves or their family, when in reality the greatest gift you can have is to *choose* to be happy -right now, right this second, in the present moment.

Your loved ones deserve and need your time, whether they know and say it or not. What better way to spend the present than with your beloved family and friends? After all, no one on their deathbed has ever said that they should've invested more time in their work than in their family. Money and a successful career can't hug you back and neither can they wipe your tears away or listen to your problems. Spend time with the ones you love and your present will be well lived.

Create New Relationships

Meeting new people is also a great way to live in the present. There will always be space for new people in your life, so don't limit yourself to just a couple of friends or a few relatives. If you're not much of an extrovert, you can try and be friends with your co-workers, neighbors, or classmates. You can even go to events you enjoy by searching on www.meetup.com. New relationships open new doors in your life and these opportunities help you have a more wonderful present.

Having new friends or visiting a relative you haven't seen for many years also allows you to extend love and care to other people. The more people you befriend and add in your life, the more you'll be able to see the positive transformations you've undergone and how you have impacted others' lives. You'll be given the chance to share what you have learned from your past and how you are now looking at your future.

Your friendship with these new people will expand your reach, considerably helping more people find their way in life and how they can fully live in the present too. You know how difficult it can be to go through painful experiences and be afraid of an unknown future, so the experience you once shunned is now also part of your inspiring testimony to others. You've now become a light in their darkness.

Accept What You Can't Change and Be Thankful for What You Can

Some things are unchangeable, uncontrollable, and unforeseeable, but these things keep life interesting. Instead of shirking whenever something can't be changed, embrace the unchangeable with your changeable heart. Your heart and thinking have changed since you've learned that letting go of the past and accepting what the future holds are key to being in the present. Feel the weight lifted off your shoulders as you let all the past go, and allow the future to be.

You can't control how people will perceive a situation. However, you can change the way you look at the situation. Learn and grow from it. You'll feel pain and you'll get disappointed every now and then because life isn't perfect as the people in it are nowhere near perfection. Be thankful that you're still alive and breathing, and have the opportunity to begin a new life looking through the perspective of *being in the present.* Live life in the present and let go of the past. Learn what you can in the present by being in the moment; and watch as the future unfolds.

Conclusion

I hope you enjoyed this book and that you are now able to see the benefits of living in the present; and most of all, I hope you've taken the strategies throughout the book and begun to apply them to your life because life is meant to be enjoyed- not full of stress and worry.

Once again, thank you for downloading this book! If you enjoyed it, please take the time to share your thoughts and post a review on Amazon. It'd be greatly appreciated!

Thank you and good luck on your journey in life!

- Matt Morris

About The Author

Matt Morris is a Certified Professional Co-Active Life Coach (CPCC). He graduated in 2006 with a Bachelors Degree in Marketing with a minor in Psychology. Since 2010, he has followed his passion and become a Life Coach who works with individuals who are married (or in relationships) with people who are addicted to drugs and/or alcohol. He helps guide them to new perspectives, rediscover themselves, and offers them strategies to move forward with their lives, despite being in a Co-Dependent relationship. To learn more, please visit: http://www.rootscoaching.com

Recommended Books:

1.

[How To Live In The Present Moment: Let Go Of The Past & Stop Worrying About The Future](#)

2.

[*Do* Talk To Strangers: A Creative, Sexy, and Fun Way To Have Emotionally Stimulating Conversations With Anyone](#)

3.

50 Places You Need To See Before You Die: A List Of The Earth's Most Beautiful, Captivating, & Eye-Catching Wonders Of The World

4.

The Power of NLP - Attract More Wealth, Better Health, And Improve Relationships

5.

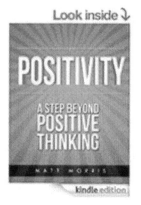

Positivity: A Step Beyond Positive Thinking

6.

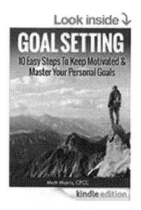

Goal Setting: 10 Easy Steps To Keep Motivated & Master Your Personal Goals

7.

The Storytelling Method: Steps To Maximize A Story And Make It Powerful, Inspiring, And Unforgettable

8.

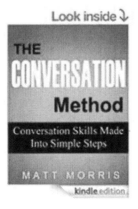

The Conversation Method: Conversation Skills Made Into Simple Steps

9.

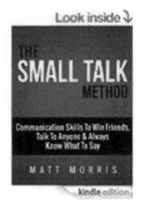

<u>**Small Talk Method: Communication Skills To Win Friends, Talk To Anyone & Always Know What To Say**</u>

10.

<u>**Emotional Intelligence: Understand Emotional Intelligence To Improve Self Management and Increase Your Social Skills**</u>

11.

<u>Codependency Gone For Good: How To Stop
Worrying, Stop Controlling, & Put Yourself First</u>

Made in the USA
Monee, IL
30 September 2020